Nat

Or the Science of Justice: A Treatise on Natural Law,
Natural Justice, Natural Rights, Natural Liberty, and Natural
Society; showing that all Legislation whatsoever is an
Absurdity, a Usurpation, and a Crime.

By
Lysander Spooner

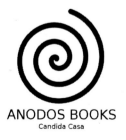

ANODOS BOOKS
Candida Casa

Lysander Spooner (1808–1887)
Originally published in 1882.
Editing, cover, and internal design by Alisdair MacNoravaich for Anodos Books.
Copyright © 2018 Anodos Books. All rights reserved.

Anodos Books
1c Kings Road
Whithorn
Newton Stewart
Dumfries & Galloway
DG8 8PP

Contents

Chapter I The Science of Justice.

The science of mine and thine—the science of justice—is the science of all human rights; of all a man's rights of person and property; of all his rights to life, liberty, and the pursuit of happiness.

It is the science which alone can tell any man what he can, and cannot, do; what he can, and cannot, have; what he can, and cannot, say, without infringing the rights of any other person.

It is the science of peace; and the only science of peace; since it is the science which alone can tell us on what conditions mankind can live in peace, or ought to live in peace, with each other.

These conditions are simply these: viz., first, that each man shall do, towards every other, all that justice requires him to do; as, for example, that he shall pay his debts, that he shall return borrowed or stolen property to its owner, and that he shall make reparation for any injury he may have done to the person or property of another.

The second condition is, that each man shall abstain from doing, to another, anything which justice forbids him to do; as, for example, that he shall abstain from committing theft, robbery arson, murder, or any other crime against the person or property of another.

So long as these conditions are fulfilled, men are at peace,

1

and ought to remain at peace, with each other. But when either of these conditions is violated, men are at war. And they must necessarily remain at war until justice is re-established.

Through all time, so far as history informs us, wherever mankind have attempted to live in peace with each other, both the natural instincts, and the collective wisdom of the human race, have acknowledged and prescribed, as an indispensable condition, obedience to this one only universal obligation: viz., *that each should live honestly towards every other.*

The ancient maxim makes the sum of a man's *legal* duty to his fellow men to be simply this: "*To live honestly, to hurt no one, to give to every one his due.*"

This entire maxim is really expressed in the single words, *to live honestly;* since to live honestly is to hurt no one, and give to every one his due.

Section II.

Man, no doubt, owes many other *moral* duties to his fellow men; such as to feed the hungry, clothe the naked, shelter the homeless, care for the sick, protect the defenceless, assist the weak, and enlighten the ignorant. But these are simply moral duties, of which each man must be his own judge, in each particular case, as to whether, and how, and how far, he can, or will, perform them. But of his *legal* duty—that is, of his duty to live honestly towards his fellow men—his fellow men not only *may* judge, but, for their own protection, *must* judge. And, if need be, they may rightfully *compel* him to perform it. They may do this, acting singly, or in concert. They may do it on the instant, as the necessity arises, or deliberately and systematically, if they prefer to do so, and the exigency will admit of it.

Although it is the right of anybody and everybody—of any one man, or set of men, no less than another—to repel injustice, and compel justice, for themselves, and for all who may be wronged, yet to avoid the errors that are liable to result from haste and passion, and that everybody, who desires it, may rest secure in the assurance of protection, without a resort to force, it is evidently desirable that men should associate, so far as they freely and voluntarily can do so, for the maintenance of justice among themselves, and for mutual protection against other wrongdoers. It is also in the highest degree desirable that they should agree upon some plan or system of judicial proceedings, which, in the trial of causes, should secure caution, deliberation, thorough investigation, and, as far as possible, freedom from every influence but the simple desire to do justice.

Yet such associations can be rightful and desirable only in so far as they are purely voluntary. No man can rightfully be coerced into joining one, or supporting one, against his will. His own interest, his own judgment, and his own conscience alone must determine whether he will join this association, or that; or whether he will join any. If he chooses to depend, for the protection of his own rights, solely upon himself, and upon such voluntary assistance as other persons may freely offer to him when the necessity for it arises, he has a perfect right to do so. And this course would be a reasonably safe one for him to follow, so long as he himself should manifest the ordinary readiness of mankind, in like cases, to go to the assistance and defence of injured persons; and should also himself "live honestly, hurt no one, and give to every one his due." For such a man is reasonably sure of always having friends and defenders enough in case of need, whether he shall have joined any association, or not.

Certainly no man can rightfully be required to join, or support, an association whose protection he does not desire.

Nor can any man be reasonably or rightfully expected to join, or support, any association whose plans, or method of proceeding, he does not approve, as likely to accomplish its professed purpose of maintaining justice, and at the same time itself avoid doing injustice. To join, or support, one that would, in his opinion, be inefficient, would be absurd. To join or support one that, in his opinion, would itself do injustice, would be criminal. He must, therefore, be left at the same liberty to join, or not to join, an association for this purpose, as for any other, according as his own interest, discretion, or conscience shall dictate.

An association for mutual protection against injustice is like an association for mutual protection against fire or shipwreck. And there is no more right or reason in *compelling* any man to join or support one of these associations, against his will, his judgment, or his conscience, than there is in compelling him to join or support any other, whose benefits (if it offer any) he does not want, or whose purposes or methods he does not approve.

SECTION IV.

No objection can be made to these voluntary associations upon the ground that they would lack that knowledge of justice, as a science, which would be necessary to enable them to maintain justice, and themselves avoid doing injustice. Honesty, justice, natural law, is usually a very plain and simple matter, easily understood by common minds. Those who desire to know what it is, in any particular case, seldom have to go far to find it. It is true, it must be learned, like any other science. But it is also true that it is very easily learned. Although as illimitable in its applications as the infinite relations and dealings of men with each other, it is, nevertheless, made up of a few simple elementary principles, of the truth and justice of which every ordinary mind has an almost intuitive perception. And almost all men have the same perceptions of what constitutes justice, or of what

4

justice requires, when they understand alike the facts from which their inferences are to be drawn.

Men living in contact with each other, and having intercourse together, *cannot avoid* learning natural law, to a very great extent, even if they would. The dealings of men with men, their separate possessions and their individual wants, and the disposition of every man to demand, and insist upon, whatever he believes to be his due, and to resent and resist all invasions of what he believes to be his rights, are continually forcing upon their minds the questions, Is this act just? or is it unjust? Is this thing mine? or is it his? And these are questions of natural law; questions which, in regard to the great mass of cases, are answered alike by the human mind everywhere.[1]

Children learn the fundamental principles of natural law at a very early age. Thus they very early understand that one child must not, without just cause, strike, or otherwise hurt, another; that one child must not assume any arbitrary control or domination over another; that one child must not, either by force, deceit, or stealth, obtain possession of anything that belongs to another; that if one child commits any of these wrongs against another, it is not only the right of the injured child to resist, and, if need be, punish the wrongdoer, and compel him to make reparation, but that it is also the right, and the moral duty, of all other children, and all other persons, to assist the injured party in defending his rights, and redressing his wrongs. These are fundamental principles of natural law, which govern the most important transactions of man with man. Yet children learn them earlier than they learn that three and three are six, or five and

[1]Sir William Jones, an English judge in India, and one of the most learned judges that ever lived, learned in Asiatic as well as European law, says: "It is pleasing to remark the similarity, or, rather, the identity, of those conclusions which pure, unbiassed reason, *in all ages and nations,* seldom fails to draw, in such juridical inquiries as are not fettered and manacled by positive institutions."—*Jones on Bailments,* 133.

He means here to say that, when no law his been made in violation of justice, judicial tribunals, "in all ages and nations," have "seldom" failed to agree as to what justice is.

five ten. Their childish plays, even, could not be carried on without a constant regard to them; and it is equally impossible for persons of any age to live together in peace on any other conditions.

It would be no extravagance to say that, in most cases, if not in all, mankind at large, young and old, learn this natural law long before they have learned the meanings of the words by which we describe it. In truth, it would be impossible to make them understand the real meanings of the words, if they did not first understand the nature of the thing itself. To make them under stand the meanings of the words justice and injustice, before knowing the nature of the things themselves, would be as impossible as it would be to make them understand the meanings of the words heat and cold, wet and dry, light and darkness, white and black, one and two, before knowing the nature of the things themselves. Men necessarily must know sentiments and ideas, no less than material things, before they can know the meanings of the words by which we describe them.

Chapter II The Science of Justice (Continued)

If justice be not a natural principle, it is no principle at all. If it be not a natural principle, there is no such thing as justice. If it be not a natural principle, all that men have ever said or written about it, from time immemorial, has been said and written about that which had no existence. If it be not a natural principle, all the appeals for justice that have ever been heard, and all the struggles for justice that have ever been witnessed, have been appeals and struggles for a mere fantasy, a vagary of the imagination, and not for a reality.

If justice be not a natural principle, then there is no such thing as injustice; and all the crimes of which the world has been the scene, have been no crimes at all; but only simple events, like the falling of the rain, or the setting of the sun; events of which the victims had no more reason to complain than they had to complain of the running of the streams, or the growth of vegetation.

If justice be not a natural principle, governments (so-called) have no more right or reason to take cognizance of it, or to pretend or profess to take cognizance of it, than they have to take cognizance, or to pretend or profess to take cognizance, of any other nonentity; and all their professions of establishing justice, or of maintaining justice, or of regarding justice, are simply the mere gibberish of fools, or the frauds of imposters.

But if justice be a natural principle, then it is necessarily an immutable one; and can no more be changed—by any power inferior to that which established it—than can the law of gravitation, the laws of light, the principles of mathematics, or any other natural law or principle whatever; and all attempts or assumptions, on the part of any man or body of men—whether calling themselves governments, or by any other name—to set up their own commands, wills, pleasure, or discretion, in the place of justice, as a rule of conduct for any human being, are as much an absurdity, an usurpation, and a tyranny, as would be their attempts to set up their own commands, wills, pleasure, or discretion in the place of any and all the physical, mental, and moral laws of the universe.

Section II.

If there be any such principle as justice, it is, of necessity, a natural principle; and, as such, it is a matter of science, to be learned and applied like any other science. And to talk of either adding to, or taking from, it, by legislation, is just as false, absurd, and ridiculous as it would be to talk of adding to, or taking from, mathematics, chemistry, or any other science, by legislation.

Section III.

If there be in nature such a principle as justice, nothing can be added to, or taken from, its supreme authority by all the legislation of which the entire human race united are capable. And all the attempts of the human race, or of any portion of it, to add to, or take from, the supreme authority of justice, in any case whatever, is of no more obligation upon any single human being than is the idle wind.

Section IV.

If there be such a principle as justice, or natural law, it is the principle, or law, that tells us what rights were given to every human being at his birth; what rights are, therefore, inherent in him as a human being, necessarily remain with him during

8

life; and, however capable of being trampled upon, are incapable of being blotted out, extinguished, annihilated, or separated or eliminated from his nature as a human being, or deprived of their inherent authority or obligation.

On the other hand, if there be no such principle as justice, or natural law, then every human being came into the world utterly destitute of rights; and coming into the world destitute of rights, he must necessarily forever remain so. For if no one brings any rights with him into the world, clearly no one can ever have any rights of his own, or give any to another. And the consequence would be that mankind could never have any rights; and for them to talk of any such things as their rights, would be to talk of things that never had, never will have, and never can have an existence.

Section V.

If there be such a natural principle as justice, it is necessarily the highest, and consequently the only and universal, law for all those matters to which it is naturally applicable. And, consequently, all human legislation is simply and always an assumption of authority and dominion, where no right of authority or dominion exists. It is, therefore, simply and always an intrusion, an absurdity, an usurpation, and a crime.

On the other hand, if there be no such natural principle as justice, there can be no such thing as injustice. If there be no such natural principle as honesty, there can be no such thing as dishonesty; and no possible act of either force or fraud, committed by one man against the person or property of another, can be said to be unjust or dishonest; or be complained of, or prohibited, or punished as such. In short, if there be no such principle as justice, there can be no such acts as crimes; and all the professions of governments, so called, that they exist, either in whole or in part, for the punishment or prevention of crimes, are professions that they exist for the punishment or prevention of what never existed, nor ever can exist. Such professions are therefore confessions that, so far as crimes are concerned, governments have no occasion to exist; that there is nothing for them to do, and that there is nothing that they can do. They are confessions that the governments exist for the punishment and prevention of acts that are, in their nature, simple impossibilities.

Section VI.

If there be in nature such a principle as justice, such a principle as honesty, such principles as we describe by the words mine and thine, such principles as men's natural rights of person and property, then we have an immutable and universal law; a law that we can learn, as we learn any other science; a law that is paramount to, and excludes, every thing that conflicts with it; a law that tells us what is just and what is unjust, what is honest and what is dishonest, what things are mine and what things are thine, what are my rights of person and property and what are your rights of person and property, and where is the boundary between each and all of my rights of person and property and each and all of your rights of person and property. And this law is the paramount law, and the same law, over all the world, at all times, and for all peoples; and will be the same paramount and only law, at all times, and for all peoples, so long as man shall live upon the earth.

But if, on the other hand, there be in nature no such principle as justice, no such principle as honesty, no such principle as men's natural rights of person or property, then all such words as justice and injustice, honesty and dishonesty, all such words as mine and thine, all words that signify that one thing is one man's property and that another thing is another man's property, all words that are used to describe men's natural rights of person or property, all such words as are used to describe injuries and crimes, should be

10

struck out of all human languages as having no meanings; and it should be declared, at once and forever, that the greatest force and the greatest frauds, for the time being, are the supreme and only laws for governing the relations of men with each other; and that, from henceforth, all persons and combinations of persons—those that call themselves governments, as well as all others—are to be left free to practice upon each other all the force, and all the fraud, of which they are capable.

Section VII.

If there be no such science as justice, there can be no science of government; and all the rapacity and violence, by which, in all ages and nations, a few confederated villains have obtained the mastery over the rest of mankind, reduced them to poverty and slavery, and established what they called governments to keep them in subjection, have been as legitimate examples of government as any that the world is ever to see.

Section VIII.

If there be in nature such a principle as justice, it is necessarily the only *political* principle there ever was, or ever will be. All the other so-called political principles, which men are in the habit of inventing, are not principles at all. They are either the mere conceits of simpletons, who imagine they have discovered something better than truth, and justice, and universal law; or they are mere devices and pretences, to which selfish and knavish men resort as means to get fame, and power, and money.

Chapter III Natural Law Contrasted With Legislation.

Natural law, natural justice, being a principle that is naturally applicable and adequate to the rightful settlement of every possible controversy that can arise among men; being, too, the only standard by which any controversy whatever, between man and man, can be rightfully settled; being a principle whose protection every man demands for himself, whether he is willing to accord it to others, or not; being also an immutable principle, one that is always and everywhere the same, in all ages and nations; being self-evidently necessary in all times and places; being so entirely impartial and equitable towards all; so indispensable to the peace of mankind everywhere; so vital to the safety and welfare of every human being; being, too, so easily learned, so generally known, and so easily maintained by such voluntary associations as all honest men can readily and rightfully form for that purpose—being such a principle as this, these questions arise, viz.: Why is it that it does not universally, or well nigh universally, prevail? Why is it that it has not, ages ago, been established throughout the world as the one only law that any man, or all men, could rightfully be compelled to obey? Why is it that any human being ever conceived that anything so self-evidently superfluous, false, absurd, and atrocious as all legislation necessarily must be, could be of any use to mankind, or have any place in human affairs?

13

The answer is, that through all historic times, wherever any people have advanced beyond the savage state, and have learned to increase their means of subsistence by the cultivation of the soil, a greater or less number of them have associated and organized themselves as robbers, to plunder and enslave all others, who had either accumulated any property that could be seized, or had shown, by their labor, that they could be made to contribute to the support or pleasure of those who should enslave them.

These bands of robbers, small in number at first, have increased their power by uniting with each other, inventing warlike weapons, disciplining themselves, and perfecting their organizations as military forces, and dividing their plunder (including their captives) among themselves, either in such proportions as have been previously agreed on, or in such as their leaders (always desirous to increase the number of their followers) should prescribe.

The success of these bands of robbers was an easy thing, for the reason that those whom they plundered and enslaved were comparatively defenceless; being scattered thinly over the country; engaged wholly in trying, by rude implements and heavy labor, to extort a subsistence from the soil; having no weapons of war, other than sticks and stones; having no military discipline or organization, and no means of concentrating their forces, or acting in concert, when suddenly attacked. Under these circumstances, the only alternative left them for saving even their lives, or the lives of their families, was to yield up not only the crops they had gathered, and the lands they had cultivated, but themselves and their families also as slaves.

Thenceforth their fate was, as slaves, to cultivate for others the lands they had before cultivated for themselves. Being driven constantly to their labor, wealth slowly increased; but

14

all went into the hands of their tyrants.

These tyrants, living solely on plunder, and on the labor of their slaves, and applying all their energies to the seizure of still more plunder, and the enslavement of still other defenceless persons; increasing, too, their numbers, perfecting their organizations, and multiplying their weapons of war, they extend their conquests until, in order to hold what they have already got, it becomes necessary for them to act systematically, and co operate with each other in holding their slaves in subjection.

But all this they can do only by establishing what they call a government, and making what they call laws.

All the great governments of the world—those now existing, as well as those that have passed away—have been of this character. They have been mere bands of robbers, who have associated for purposes of plunder, conquest, and the enslavement of their fellow men. And their laws, as they have called them, have been only such agreements as they have found it necessary to enter into, in order to maintain their organizations, and act together in plundering and enslaving others, and in securing to each his agreed share of the spoils.

All these laws have had no more real obligation than have the agreements which brigands, bandits, and pirates find it necessary to enter into with each other, for the more successful accomplishment of their crimes, and the more peaceable division of their spoils.

Thus substantially all the legislation of the world has had its origin in the desires of one class of persons to plunder and enslave others, *and hold them as property.*

Section III.

In process of time, the robber, or slave holding, class—who had seized all the lands, and held all the means of creating

15

wealth—began to discover that the easiest mode of managing their slaves, and making them profitable, was *not* for each slaveholder to hold his specified number of slaves, as he had done before, and as he would hold so many cattle, but to give them so much liberty as would throw upon themselves (the slaves) the responsibility of their own subsistence, and yet compel them to sell their labor to the land-holding class—their former owners—for just what the latter might choose to give them.

Of course, these liberated slaves, as some have erroneously called them, having no lands, or other property, and no means of obtaining an independent subsistence, had no alternative—to save themselves from starvation—but to sell their labor to the landholders, in exchange only for the coarsest necessaries of life; not always for so much even as that.

These liberated slaves, as they were called, were now scarcely less slaves than they were before. Their means of subsistence were perhaps even more precarious than when each had his own owner, who had an interest to preserve his life. They were liable, at the caprice or interest of the land-holders, to be thrown out of home, employment, and the opportunity of even earning a subsistence by their labor. They were, therefore, in large numbers, driven to the necessity of begging, stealing, or starving; and became, of course, dangerous to the property and quiet of their late masters.

The consequence was, that these late owners found it necessary, for their own safety and the safety of their property, to organize themselves more perfectly as a government, *and make laws for keeping these dangerous people in subjection;* that is, laws fixing the prices at which they should be compelled to labor, and also prescribing fearful punishments, even death itself, for such thefts and trespasses as they were driven to commit, as their only means of saving themselves from starvation.

16

These laws have continued in force for hundreds, and, in some countries, for thousands of years; and are in force to-day, in greater or less severity, in nearly all the countries on the globe.

The purpose and effect of these laws have been to maintain, in the hands of the robber, or slave holding class, a monopoly of all lands, and, as far as possible, of all other means of creating wealth; and thus to keep the great body of laborers in such a state of poverty and dependence, as would compel them to sell their labor to their tyrants for the lowest prices at which life could be sustained.

The result of all this is, that the little wealth there is in the world is all in the hands of a few—that is, in the hands of the law-making, slave-holding class; who are now as much slave-holders in spirit as they ever were, but who accomplish their purposes by means of *the laws they make* for keeping the laborers in subjection and dependence, instead of each one's owning his individual slaves as so many chattels.

Thus the whole business of legislation, which has now grown to such gigantic proportions, had its origin in the conspiracies, which have always existed among the few, for the purpose of holding the many in subjection, and extorting from them their labor, and all the profits of their labor.

And the real motives and spirit which lie at the foundation of all legislation—notwithstanding all the pretences and disguises by which they attempt to hide themselves—are the same to-day as they always have been. The whole purpose of this legislation is simply to keep one class of men in subordination and servitude to another.

SECTION IV.

What, then, is legislation? It is an assumption by one man, or body of men, of absolute, irresponsible dominion over all other men whom they can subject to their power. It is the

17

assumption by one man, or body of men, of a right to subject all other men to their will and their service. It is the assumption by one man, or body of men, of a right to abolish outright all the natural rights, all the natural liberty of all other men; to make all other men their slaves; to arbitrarily dictate to all other men what they may, and may not, do; what they may, and may not, have; what they may, and may not, be. It is, in short, the assumption of a right to banish the principle of human rights, the principle of justice itself, from off the earth, and set up their own personal will, pleasure, and interest in its place. All this, and nothing less, is involved in the very idea that there can be any such thing as human legislation that is obligatory upon those upon whom it is imposed.

Made in United States
North Haven, CT
14 April 2022

18234725R00015